Road Trip

Road Trip

K. Blouin

Road Trip

Copywrite © 2019 by Kelsey Blouin

All rights reserved. This book or any portion thereof may not be reproduced or used in any manner whatsoever without the express written permission of the publisher except for the use of brief quotations in a book review.

Printed in Canada

First Printing, 2019

ISBN 978-1-9995661-0-4

Cover design by Shawna Motuzas

Interior design by Kelsey Blouin

Road Trip

Thank you

To the strongest woman I know,

Thank you for allowing me to see a pure definition of independence. Not a day goes by that I do not face the world with kindness and without wearing my heart on my sleeve. If I can be half the mom you are, I'll know I've done something right.

To the friends that keep me wild,

Thank you for keeping me on my toes. They say you know who your true friends are throughout the phases of your life. Amazingly enough, I have known all of you throughout the majority of mine. Blessed does not even begin to describe how I feel to have you all by my side throughout this journey we call life.

To those who broke my heart and the others who helped mend it,

Know that I am forever grateful to you. You cannot take the highs without the lows, and I do not think I would have wanted it any other way.

To everyone that reached out to me throughout the process of me putting this together,

Thank you for believing in me and for pushing me to be the absolute truest version of myself.

Lastly,

To every reader who had their heart shattered and still finds themselves picking up the pieces. To those that, despite their experiences, continue to choose love without fear or expectation.

This one is for you. This one is for us.

Road Trip

Road Trip

You

As you read
the feelings
I have transformed
into words
and the memories
I have transformed
into sentences
I know they will
scream
your name.

I can only hope that
with time
you will allow
your guilt
to turn into reflection,
your pain
to turn into strength
and your mistakes
to turn into lessons.

For I've
wept for the
nights I no longer
want to remember
and the days I
forcibly try to forget
and with that
I've learned
that forgiving you
was the key
to setting myself free.

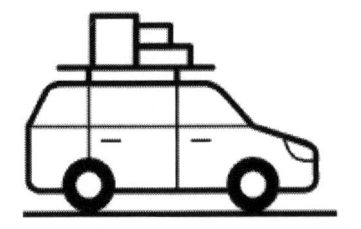

Road Trip

Road Trip

Chapter One

You Promised.

You Lied.

I left.

Road Trip

Qualities

I cannot help
but give someone
the benefit of the doubt
despite their constant contradictions.

Finding the best in people
has become
my greatest triumph
as well as my most destructive pursuit.

Road Trip

Silent Clues

She warned you
that her eyes
were a window
to her soul
and you were
smart enough
to listen.

So despite the lies
she commits to tell
you already see
the truth.

Road Trip

High School Sweet Hearts

As a teen, I was handed a free pass of acceptance.

While everyone was searching for themselves
I was being fed words of encouragement,
promises of fulfillment,
and dreams of the future.

I was being led
blindly through the days
and emotionally through the years.

As an adult, I was taught a lesson of rejection.

While everyone found themselves,
I had always only found you.

Road Trip

Second Guess

Asking myself
where we stand
instead of knowing
is the sole
driving force
behind me
walking away.

Road Trip

Moved On

I spoke and you continued
to ignore the truth.

Despite loving you for
all that you were
I no longer love you
for all that you are.

Road Trip

Sold

Two names
anxiously signed
across a thinly dotted line.

One of them
doesn't want
to be there,
silently screaming
to be released.

The other sits
with false assumptions
that this is
the only
solution.

They both
tell the same lie
and decorate it with
a legal obligation
and a financial commitment.

Road Trip

No Vacancy

For this house
was crafted on
blind eyes and
beating hearts.

It was painted with
long nights and
amateur promises.

It was furnished with
ambitious dreams and
undeniable pride.

However, this house
was broken with
lingering eyes and
the opening of a door
that was meant to remain closed.

Road Trip

Latch

The idea of who
you could have become
always kept me
latched on.

I believed in you
even when you didn't
believe in yourself.

Road Trip

Liar

Blindsided and
torn to shreds
with an excuse of
unknowing affection and
misplaced emotion.

Road Trip

Dishonesty

Somewhere
mixed in
with your
words and
trapped
between
the lines
I found the
truth
that set me
free.

Road Trip

Communication

Guilty
for the nights
I couldn't
tell you how I
really felt,
knowing
it was slowly
destroying us.

Somehow
that presented itself
as the only
solution
but really,
it was a
defining
problem.

Road Trip

Selfish

When they ask
you what happened

Tell them how
you had to put out my fire
before you could ignite your own.

Explain how you
robbed my time and
filled me with promises of
a better tomorrow

All while your fingers
were crossed in a pitiful
attempt to protect
your image.

Road Trip

Consequence of Heartbreak

You didn't
build a wall
you built
a house.

You let people in
but you never
let them stay.

Road Trip

Directions

Look right
into what is left
and then tell me
you do not know
what your next move
needs to be.

Road Trip

Power

Waves hit the shore
like the truth hit
the surface.

Strong and without
restriction.

Road Trip

Home

Because how can
something so
significant
be defined by
some place
that can be
taken away at
any moment.

Road Trip

Fact

You never once asked
if I wanted to stay.

I asked you
to leave my life
not your responsibilities.

Road Trip

The same boy

My heart broke
when you walked
out the door.

It shattered
when my best friend
left with him.

Road Trip

Lesson

Never underestimate the power of clearly defined expectations with actions that do not follow suit.

It will break your heart every time.

Road Trip

Fine

She wears her broken smile
that everyone
believes to be true.

She hides her tired eyes
that everyone
believe to be honest.

She owns her pale complexion
that everyone
believes to be a result of her day.

She lies about her shattered heart
that everyone
believes to be mended.

She acts like the girl
she was before her whole world
completely shifted
when you walked out the door.

Road Trip

Heal

You removed
my heart
from my chest
and buried it
with shame.

I dug through the
anger,
pain,
suffering,
and pulled out
a piece
each time.

Road Trip

Anxiety

How does the silence of the night
turn into an overwhelming
period of self-doubt
and reflections on
unanswered questions?

Why when I'm able to shut off
and silence the world,
can I still not manage
to even begin to quiet you…

Road Trip

My choice

When they ask you
what happened
I hope you tell them

how your presence vanished
in the blink of an eye

how your heart broke and
how you lost too many pieces
to be able to repair

how your eyes turned cold
and stopped looking for joy.

But mostly,

I hope you tell them

how instead of dealing
with your own suffering
you transferred it on to the
one person, who despite it all
still
chose
you
everyday.

Road Trip

Cry

I might act like
cutting you out
of my life was easy.

But my pillow would say otherwise.

Road Trip

254

The walls echo with
the stories of yesterday.

If they had a voice
the secrets they could broadcast and
the lies they could uncover
would be enough to destroy you.

Road Trip

It's Okay

Release the tears
that you have been
holding back with
your self-depriving
definition of
strength.

Road Trip

Depression

It hovers.
Heavy, strong and passionate.
Relentless,
in its pursuit.

When faced,
it never trembles.
For it,
is the calm before the storm.

It leaves us longing
waiting, wishing
for even just a moment
without it.

It is behind every
what-if question
whose answer is based on an
underlying sense of failure.

It is behind every
brave encounter.
A decision made to take a chance.
To put it aside for the opportunity,
the possibility.

It can persuade
even the strongest to lose sight.
To lose themselves.

Road Trip

Sad

They say
you are only
as happy as
your saddest child.

So tell me mom
where does that leave you?

Road Trip

Games

My eyes detect
the truth that
my heart
doesn't want to feel and
my brain
doesn't want me to
understand.

And although I see,
I can't help but remain
blind to the feelings
that continue to
corrupt my thoughts
and shatter my expectations.

Road Trip

Second Chance

I watched as
you provided me
with every piece of
evidence I needed
to move on.

Road Trip

Guarded

I've learned
that anyone
who you allow
close enough to see
a genuine piece
of your soul
can break your heart
and that's terrifying.

Road Trip

Blues

I'll never truly learn
how to deal with
the men
who fall in love
with the
color of my eyes
rather than
the color of my soul.

Road Trip

Can't Sleep

Through words unsaid
and actions misinterpreted,
I've learned the most unrecognized
form of self-destruction.

- *I've learned how to break my own heart.*

Road Trip

Rules

I tried to be
the exception
to your rule and it
ended with me being
played the same as
those before me.

Turns out
your rules are
a cop out
for not being honest
and an excuse
for being cruel.

Road Trip

Choose Me

Remember
when you told me
I was
everything
you
needed.

Forgetting
that I only ever
needed
to be
everything
you
wanted.

Road Trip

Tender

She loved you
with ease
even when you loved her
with distance.

Road Trip

Internal Alarm

My anxiety always
knows before I do.

Like a heavyset warning
it will speed up my heart
and place a weight on my chest.

Like a perfectly timed indicator
that something beyond my control,
with an overcasting impact,
has entered my life and
will need to be dealt with.

Road Trip

Deceit

You can't expect me
to not have all these feelings
when you kiss me like
you're scared to lose me.

Road Trip

Lonely

She was kept in the dark
by the one person she could trust
to help her find her light.

Road Trip

Communicate

Tell her the
truth.

So at least
when she can't
sleep
at night
she has a
reason
why.

Road Trip

3:17 AM

I love that
I don't need
to answer
to anyone
but myself.

However,
when the night gets long
and time seems to halt
I wish I wanted to.

Road Trip

Pretend

How can you
look at me
as if the idea of us didn't exist?

As if the way
you kissed me
and the way
you held me
wasn't real at all?

And if this was nothing
all along, look at me
in the eyes and recite
the words you chose to
write and send in the middle of the night.

That's right, I didn't
think you could either.

Road Trip

Protect your Image

Your obsession behind
your untouched reputation and
senseless vulnerability
holds the key to the answers
that you are so desperately
searching to discover
but too foolishly
blind to see.

Road Trip

Free

Liberate yourself
from
the shackles
of your pride
and the
burden
of your ego.

Road Trip

Broke

He offered me something
I could not refuse
for something
I promised myself
I'd never sell.

Road Trip

Explanation Needed

Why leave me
on the fence
and then
complain
that I'm so far.

Why push me
to the side
and then
complain
that I'm not around.

Why play these games
in the first place
and then wonder
why I'm so far gone.

Road Trip

Thought You Were Different

You solidified
that I wasn't worth
the wait with
your excuses.

You clarified
that you weren't worth
the time I spent
thinking you were.

Road Trip

Pondering

She held her verdict by a string
and dangled it along her path of reflection
as I chased for an answer to a problem
only she knew existed.

Road Trip

You Already Know

You carry
secrets
that have shaped me,
emotions
that have broken me,
and feelings
that continue to punish me.

To this day,
I'm still not sure if
you even know
to what extent you
destroyed me.

Road Trip

Woman at 9

The fabrication of
my womanhood
wasn't an invitation
to destroy my
childhood.

The one thing
I was allowed to have
for myself
and it was stolen
at the hands
of those who
were supposed to
protect my innocence
and preserve my youth.

Road Trip

Waves

Lost at sea
my mind got
used to the chaos
of the waves being

angry at the night sky
for its presence,

angry at the depth below
for its unknowingly calm composition,

angry at the way factors outside of their control
impact their entire make up.

Road Trip

Walls

What hurts
the most
is that I
allowed
myself
to get
excited
about
you.

Road Trip

Empath

Some people are given
so much love that
despite their want to feel nothing
they cannot help but feel it all.

Road Trip

Grow Up

I can no longer
concern myself
with a man,
who despite being
in constant pursuit,
refuses
to love in return.

Road Trip

No Explanation Needed

It's a selfish thing to do
to take responsibility
for something
just to be
a part of it.

Road Trip

Hypocrite

Some people keep telling me
that the person I end up with
will not leave me wondering
about how they feel about me.

It's funny because
half the time
I wonder how
they do.

Road Trip

Move Along

You make her
beg for attention
like the dog
you never had.

Not understanding
that the right girl
will never have to
beg in the first place.

Road Trip

Fool

Turns out
what I thought
I wanted
was simply
my heart
craving
the rhythm
of another.

The synchronized
harmony of companionship
rang louder
than my desire
for simplicity.

Road Trip

Stop

Stop telling me how
great I am
as if that can erase
the way your words
rolled off your tongue
and punctured my walls.

As if it can take back the time
I spent wanting you,
thinking about you.

Road Trip

Wide Awake

Say the words
that you tuck into
bed with you
at two a.m.
when she's on
your mind
and you can't
fall asleep.

Road Trip

Ghosted

When we talked
for the last time,
you ended the conversation
with sweet promises of the future.

It is funny that you forgot
to mention that that future would not be with me.

Road Trip

Step Up

I didn't wake up this morning
looking for your reassurance
of how great of a person I am.

I already get that from the
choices I make,
the words I say
and the actions I display.

I was never looking for you to
justify my worth.

I was looking for you
to act on it.

Road Trip

Your Loss

It was never
the right time
and it was never
the right moment.

Then it was.

And you missed it.

Because your mind
was already made up
before I even had
a chance.

Road Trip

Truth

I learned the hard way
that it's easy
to lose yourself
to the idea of love.

You begin to accept
mediocre care and
mediocre people
to fill a void
you ultimately
created yourself.

Road Trip

I've Dealt With This Before

My heart got a blow
in public today.

A crowd surrounded me as
my knees got weak
and my face flushed red.

Without hesitation
I played it off
as a piece of my complexion
and a long day.

Road Trip

On Repeat

My expectations
have always been
the root
of my own
heartbreak.

I promise
you can't
break my heart
worse than
I already do.

Road Trip

Blend In

I taught myself
how to fade into the
darkness by
reminding myself
that shadows
mostly come out in
the sun anyways.

Road Trip

Giver

I was never alone
enough to realize
how I masked my desires
to assist others reach theirs.

Road Trip

Venom

Your words turned into venom
that would pour from your lips
each time you spoke.

Your lies turned into reasons
that would be used as ammunition
each time you called.

You were a master of manipulation
with a poisoned perspective and deadly opinion.

But love kept us blind
from the reality
of who you had become
with hopes that tomorrow,
your truth would be your antidote
from the poison you prescribed yourself.

Road Trip

Advice From Her

Put on your favourite song
and dance away your heartache.

When the music stops,
so do your tears.

Road Trip

Chapter Two

She Overcame.

She Transformed.

I Arrived.

Road Trip

Evolve

You asked me to transform myself,
so I hid amongst my truth.

A perfectly planned motion of deceit,
until you stared into the soul of a woman
transformed by her strength and persistence.

You asked me to transform back into the girl you used to
know but it was too late.

For my eyes finally stopped looking for pieces of you
when they did not recognize anything else.

Road Trip

Aside

I've become so accustom
to handling my hardships
that I forgot I also
need to face them.

Road Trip

Consistency

I measure your
commitment
on the effort
you choose to display.

Someone who
doesn't want
to lose something
won't put themselves
in a position to
in the first place.

Road Trip

Gone

You blended in
with the stars
and disappeared
into the night.

Oddly enough,
I still find myself
looking for a piece of you
amongst the constellations.

Road Trip

Set Free

Like a beam of light
you set me free
amongst the fire
knowing all along
that I would blend right in.

Road Trip

Brace Yourself

The calm after the storm
can leave you feeling empty.

When you become so used to
fighting for peace,
finally getting it
is foreign.

Road Trip

Blossomed

I hope you know
I loved you for all that you were.

Which is exactly why,
I can't associate myself with all that you are.

The girl you knew
is not the woman I am.

The times have changed
and with that, so have I.

Road Trip

Cautious

I have no problem
letting someone in.
I will even hold the
door open and welcome them.

But I also have no problem
asking them to leave.
I always forget
to shut the door
behind me anyways.

Road Trip

Him

You
will
always
be
my forbidden fruit.

A persistent reminder
that you don't always
have to
taste
something
in order to
crave
it.

Road Trip

2:00 AM

Despite learning
how to truly
embrace
my solitude,
I've never been
so lonely.

Road Trip

Bed Time

"Maybe tomorrow"
she whispers
as she unclips
her heart off her sleeve,
and tucks
herself
into bed.

Road Trip

Answer this

The monsters in her head
became scarier than the ones
under her bed.

Except these weren't
the ones you were taught
to fight.

These were the ones
you were taught to ignore.

Like the shadow you see
in the corner of your eye.

Or the footsteps you hear
in the silence of the night.

They don't exist
if you don't talk about them…

Right?

Road Trip

Missing

We searched for you
not knowing
you had
already
been
stolen.

I still search for you
knowing
you've
been
found.

Road Trip

Judgement

I've come to terms
with the fact that
people are a reflection
of how they choose to describe you
without ever getting to know you
in the first place.

Road Trip

Validate

She asked me how
she lost her strength
when that was all she ever had.

I asked her why
she was using broken
as an excuse to be weak.

Road Trip

Standards

The only fear
I can't seem to face
is the one where
I might actually
end up alone.

Road Trip

In a Rut

Your priorities are
shifted.
Your mindset is
foggy.

Your emotions are
drained.
Your strength is
missing.

Your heart beats
heavy.
Your brain is
scattered.

Your joints are
stretching.

For the change
you so desperately need.

Road Trip

New Years

We wait
for one day
of the year
for permission
to change and
to reinvent
ourselves.

Forgetting
that the only
permission you need
you already
had all along.

Road Trip

Her

Like the start
of your
favourite
song,
you sing
into the night
a tale of
endless
thoughts.

- *Listening to my best friend talk.*

Road Trip

Sail

My soul has been
lost for so long
that now that I see
the shore ahead
I do not know if I'm ready
to face the pier.

Road Trip

Lost

The moment
you lose your
sense of purpose
and look for it
in others
instead of
yourself,

Is the exact sign
that you've been waiting for
to begin loving yourself
for all that you are
and all that you will be.

Road Trip

Mistake

Without the glimmer of hope
in your eyes
her ambition stood still.

She forgot that the little things
ignited her drive and the
simple ones maintained it.

Without the reassurance
that she was enough
her world stopped.

She disregarded the fact that
being enough was never about
receiving recognition
like she completed some sort of
outstanding achievement.

Road Trip

Revelation

Through my darkness
I was able to shed
some light
on things I'd convinced
myself to be true despite
the evidence otherwise.

Road Trip

Aligned

The moon
took away her fear
and lit up her path.

As the sun rose
so did her courage,
for the universe heard her plea.

Road Trip

Alone

Ruled
by the moon
and guided
by the sun,
she journeys
on her path of
solitude.

Road Trip

Songs of the Sky

The birds chirp
a melody into the night
filling my silence
with songs of the sky
and tales of the adventurous.

Road Trip

Confetti

I sprinkle pieces of
myself like confetti
in every
place I visit,
person I meet,
and experience I share.

So tell me,
if home if where the heart is
where do I belong?

Road Trip

Misplaced

I buried my truth
to protect theirs.

Now that I'm ready to begin
piecing it all together,
I can't remember where I hid the shatters.

I hid them so well
from you,
that I lost them
for myself.

I guess that's what you get
when you decide to
make them disappear
from your mind
to avoid
consuming your heart.

It's what you get
when you decide
to prioritize everyone else's happiness
when you know
you'd strip the innocence from their eyes
with one confirmation.

Road Trip

Lies We Tell Ourselves

You peak at the past
to help you move forward.

While moving forward
you're promising yourself
you will no longer look back.

Road Trip

Reality

It wasn't until
pictures
played out as
scenes
and
statistics
became
friends
that I realized
the extent of my shelter.

Road Trip

Gamble

My mind is a slot machine
a powerful random array
of possible outcomes
that spin in my head
until finally one is
chosen as my fate.

The outcomes are never predictable
and you take many hits
before finally, randomly
you get what you have been chasing
this whole time.

Road Trip

11:11

My heart stops as
the minute ticks
and I take the moment
to be thankful for
the wishes I transformed
into goals
because when you don't
need anyone
to validate your desires
you're free to take on
any obstacle
and overcome
any challenge.

Road Trip

"You're Too Nice"

I'm told
my smile is a
continued sign
of positivity.
Capable of
captivating
a room.

I'm told
my eyes are a
vessel of honesty.
Capable of
telling
more about me
than my words.

I'm told
my laugh is infectious
and genuine.
Capable of
contaminating
others.

I'm told
my heart is
too big.
Capable of being
worn on my sleeve
free of judgement and full of pride.

You see, I'm told
all of these things
before they're taken away
with a disease like accusation
that I can never shake.

Road Trip

Math

I'm my own
equation
with a set of rules
so complex
that only few
can solve.

Road Trip

Heart of Gold

I stitched it
back together with love
and polished it off
with kindness.

I then clipped it back
onto my sleeve
where it belongs.

Road Trip

Problem

We are a generation
built on instant gratification.

We are stitched together with good intentions
and polished off with superficial expectations.

Road Trip

Setting Boundaries

It wasn't until she unshackled
the lingering guilt
of calls missed,
plans canceled and
priorities shifted
that she was able to
see clearly that her time
didn't belong to anyone
but herself.

Road Trip

Excuses

You call her
aggressive
as if your
condescending
accusations
will take away
the validity
of her argument.

Road Trip

SOS

Nice people
are the tormented.

They choose
kindness
without
expecting it in return.

They choose
love
without
expecting to fall.

They choose
to give
without
expecting to receive.

And you see,
they'll choose you
time and time again
without any expectation
that you'd ever choose them.

Road Trip

Boys vs Men

With my words
I challenge
yours with a
passionate
outcry of
equality.

My voice
erupts
with opinions
that break
stereotypes
and push
boundaries.

You attempt to
silence
me with another
conviction
of being
too loud and
too much for
any man to
handle.

You try to
manipulate
my self-worth
as if it's
a piece that
can be
owned
by another.

Road Trip

Aim High

Don't hide in fear
of what others will think.

Instead,
scare yourself
with what you didn't think
you could accomplish
but conquered anyways.

Road Trip

Adventure

My heart wasn't made
to be sedentary.

It beats a little stronger
with each adventure,
a little wiser
with each experience,
and sometimes
it even stops time.

Road Trip

Double Double

She's a strong
cup of coffee
with just the
right amount of sugar.

And although
that's not what you'd
choose to order,
it never stopped you
from taking a sip.

Road Trip

I Change Minds

A vessel of stereotypes
walked into the room
and the silence
erupts into claps
of judgement

They look at your
capacity and knowingly
decide that you take up
too much space

They look at your
composition and get
uncomfortable
in their own skin.

…

A vessel of stereotypes
walks out of the room
and shatters expectations

They look at your
smile and the way
it infectiously grows on
all that surround you

They look at your
silhouette and can now
only manage to see
your heart on your sleeve.

Road Trip

Dear Body, I'm Sorry.

I'm grateful for the days
you held me straight
as my knees grew weak.

I'm grateful for the moments
you kept breathing
when I felt like I couldn't anymore.

I'm grateful for the times
you kept my heart beating
after I felt ever piece of it shatter.

I'm grateful for the years
you withstood my hate and
continued to guide me forward.

But mostly, I'm grateful that you
could accept an apology
you never received.

Until now.

Road Trip

Worthy

To the girl who feels
like her waist line is a
reflection of her heart…

Know that the size
of your character can
never be defined
by someone's preference
of physical measurements.

Road Trip

Plus Size

Every inch,
every curve and
every imperfect mark
form a silhouette
outside of the norm
that isn't afraid of
pushing boundaries
and changing minds.

Road Trip

Goals

I celebrate being on top
by analyzing every move it took
to get me there in the first place.

Road Trip

Millennials

Your eyes feast on
the flesh of those
brave enough to
show a little skin.

You fail to realize
that your approval
was never sought and
your opinion was never required.

We're a new generation
that is not scared to be
the first to push societal norms.

We embrace ourselves
as much as we thrive
off changing minds.

So turn your head
and stare
as we walk by
and know
that you've just witnessed
a walking change.

Road Trip

Pick Us

A shot of tequila
follow by a
voice shaking,
stomach hurting,
heart screaming,
secret telling
moment of
truth.

A conversation
filled with
dreams
larger
than our
heart
can handle
alone.

Promises of
change,
growth
and a fresh
perspective.

A night
that ends with
waking up
in the morning
and erasing it all
with a
drunken excuse of
misplaced
affection.

- *That's how I told her.*

Road Trip

Garden

That's what
you wear
on your sleeve.

A heart bloomed full.

And it is the most
beautiful
thing of all.

Road Trip

Package

She stamped fragile
on her heart
so that maybe the
next one
would handle with care.

Road Trip

Storm

I'm the lightning
you'll stay up
all night to watch
and potentially
never see.

Road Trip

Real

I chose me
and because of that,
so did you.

Road Trip

Lesson

I'm confident enough
to start the conversation
because I love myself enough
to know when I should
end it.

Road Trip

Confessions of an Over Thinker

Something
about how my
words flow
so effortlessly
off my tongue
when I talk
to you
makes me do a
double take
every
time.

Road Trip

Clueless

New love
with
that old love feel.

Too
intense
to ignore.
Yet, too
familiar
to chase.

Same woman
with
a different approach.

Too
naïve
to know better.
Yet, too
hopeful
to give up.

Road Trip

Meant to be

Like two worlds
colliding into one
our paths were intertwined
by forces beyond our control.

Road Trip

Fling

I was presented everything
I had been asking for
the moment I stopped asking for it.

There I was
miles away
from the place I call home
and you managed to make me feel
like this is where I want to be.

A safe place between your arms
made me rethink everything.

Road Trip

Pick Me

I want to
be the scariest
risk
you are
willing to
take.

Road Trip

Fire

I'll ignite it
with that glance
and you'll decorate it
with a kiss.

Road Trip

Mine

I fell in
love
with your
smile
and now,
I'm part
of the
reason
you do.

Road Trip

Road Trip

I'll drive you to places
you've never been
and kiss you
until you can never forget.

Road Trip

Close

I had been in
hiding for so long that
when I was finally
nestled between
your arms
and felt free to be myself
I was terrified.

Road Trip

Kiss and Tell

The words
she couldn't
bring herself
to say
still managed
to roll off her lips
and press
onto his.

Road Trip

Last First Kiss

I long for the day
you kiss me again
and I am reminded of
how we got to be here
in the first place.

Road Trip

Tu me Manques

A piece of my heart
will always belong to the unexpected.

And that my love,
is you.

Road Trip

Falling

And when I finally
felt your hands on
my body
I realized
the extent of the
trouble
I was in.

Road Trip

Soon

I crave
the day
you grab onto me
with the same
passion
that flows
from your lips
onto mine.

Road Trip

My Morning Alarm

I will never forget the first time
I saw his eyes light up
at the sight of me in the morning
as he brushed my hair to the side.

"You're the most beautiful like this,"
he whispered and proceeded to
seal his confession with a kiss.

Road Trip

Gardener

I planted seeds of his love
in a garden I choose to nurture
because what is love if you don't
enjoy the part of watching
it all blossom before your very eyes.

Road Trip

Relationship Goals

Let me spoil
you with consistency
and the promise
that you'll never have to
second guess
how I feel about you,
how I feel about us.

Road Trip

Dirty Talk

Tell me again
how my lips
taste like sin
pressed so boldly
against yours.

Road Trip

Count Down

I crave the day
your lips touch my body
the same way I do
thinking about you.

Road Trip

Make a Move

With one touch,
I will sing your name
into the night
like your favorite song.

Road Trip

Worth the Wait

Hooked on the possibility
that tomorrow will come
and you'll continue
to choose me.

Road Trip

Ghosts

The moment I chose you,
they all decided to
begin choosing me.

Ghosts of who left
without a word
were now lining up
to pour their every thought.

Road Trip

Smoke

Puff puff pass along
the conspiracy theories that will
keep us up until the moon
kisses the horizon and
the sun awakens
the truths of tomorrow.

Road Trip

Advice

If she does not make you
want to tell her
what makes your day
a little brighter,
your heart beat
a little faster,
and the moments
that keep you up at night…

She is not the one for you.

Do not waste her time.

Road Trip

Whisper

You whispered away
the worries that were triggered
by the ghosts of those before you.

You kissed away
the fears that lingered
and refused to let them push you out.

I had given my thoughts
the power to destroy everything around me
until you loved me in a way
that allowed me to understand,
that I had to save me from myself.

Road Trip

A letter to the lonely

When you reach a certain
point in your life
where you still
haven't learned
how to properly love
another person,
you need to let someone teach you
or bask in your solitude

Wasting someone's time
for temporary fulfillment
is selfish
and ultimately
benefits no one.
Either get with the times
or get left behind.

We're a new generation
that is over
the excuse
of a good time over
a good person

We've beaten
all the levels and
realized the game
is a continuous re-enactment
of your own fears –

and we're not scared anymore

So love
and be loved,
or leave us all alone.

Road Trip

Remember

I've turned
people,
places,
feelings
into poetry.

Sometimes
although I can't
speak my truth
I sure as hell can write it.

Road Trip

Index

#.
2:00 AM	90
3:17 AM	49
11:11	112
254	33

A.
A letter to the lonely	161
Adventurer	122
Advice	159
Advice from Her	78
Aim High	121
Aligned	104
Alone	105
Answer This	92
Anxiety	30
Aside	82

B.
Bed Time	91
Blend In	75
Blossomed	87
Blues	40
Boys vs Men	120
Brace Yourself	86
Broke	53

C.
Can't Sleep	41
Cautious	88

Road Trip

Choose Me	43
Close	144
Clueless	137
Communicate	48
Communication	19
Confessions of an over thinker	136
Confetti	107
Consequence of Heartbreak	21
Consistency	83
Count Down	154
Cry	32

D.

Dear Body, I'm Sorry	125
Deceit	46
Depression	35
Directions	22
Dirty Talk	153
Dishonesty	18
Double Double	123

E.

Empath	61
Evolve	81
Excuses	118
Explanation Needed	54

F.

Fact	25
Falling	148
Fine	28

Fire	141
Fling	139
Fool	66
Free	52

G.
Gamble	111
Games	37
Garden	131
Gardener	151
Ghosted	69
Ghosts	157
Giver	76
Goals	128
Gone	84
Grow Up	62
Guarded	39

H.
Heal	29
Heart of Gold	115
Her	99
High School Sweet Hearts	11
Him	89
Home	24
Hypocrite	64

I.
I Change Minds	124
In a Rut	97
Internal Alarm	45

Its Ok	34
I've dealt with this before	73

J.
Judgement	94

K.
Kiss and Tell	145

L.
Last First Kiss	146
Latch	16
Lesson	27
Lesson	135
Liar	17
Lies we tell ourselves	109
Lonely	47
Lost	101

M.
Make a Move	155
Math	114
Meant to be	138
Millennials	129
Mine	142
Misplaced	108
Missing	93
Mistake	102
Move Along	65
Moved On	13
My Choice	31

Road Trip

My Morning Alarm　　　　　150

N.
New Years　　　　　　　　98
No Explanation Needed　　　63
No Vacancy　　　　　　　　15

O.
On Repeat　　　　　　　　74

P.
Package　　　　　　　　　132
Pick Me　　　　　　　　　140
Pick Us　　　　　　　　　130
Plus Size　　　　　　　　127
Pondering　　　　　　　　56
Power　　　　　　　　　　23
Pretend　　　　　　　　　50
Problem　　　　　　　　　116
Protect Your Image　　　　51

Q.
Qualities　　　　　　　　　9

R.
Real　　　　　　　　　　　134
Reality　　　　　　　　　　110
Relationship Goals　　　　　152
Remember　　　　　　　　162
Revelation　　　　　　　　103
Road Trip　　　　　　　　143

Road Trip

Rules	42

S.

Sad	36
Sail	100
Second Chance	38
Second Guess	12
Selfish	20
Set free	85
Setting Boundaries	117
Silent Clues	10
Smoke	158
Sold	14
Songs of the Sky	106
Soon	149
SOS	119
Standards	96
Step Up	70
Stop	67
Storm	133

T.

Tender	44
The Same Boy	26
Thought you were different	55
Truth	72
Tu me Manques	147

V.

Validate	95
Venom	77

W.
Walls	60
Waves	59
Whisper	160
Wide Awake	68
Woman at 9	58
Worth the Wait	156
Worthy	127

Y.
You	5
You Already Know	57
Your Loss	71
You're Too Nice	113